Your Heart's Voice

Renée Greene Murphy MS Ed

Fulton Books
Meadville, PA

Published by Fulton Books 2023

ISBN 979-8-88731-928-5 (paperback)
ISBN 979-8-89221-011-9 (hardcover)
ISBN 979-8-88731-929-2 (digital)

Printed in the United States of America

To my beloved little brother, Robert.
You will forever live on through us.
Your magnetic light will continue to guide us,
teach us and comfort us.

"Jade, when you are finished playing, please clean up before you leave the room you are playing in. I have asked you many times. I almost tripped on your dolls," said Mom.

1

"Okay," Jade replied. *Why does Mom always expect me to clean up MY mess? After all, she is the mom*, she thought with a snarky face. The peculiar voice in her heart told her to put her dolls away before she left the den, but she was in a hurry and decided not to.

Jade went back into her room to color, as coloring often helped her mind to relax. She was in the middle of coloring a beautiful picture of an angel that she drew for her uncle. She had promised him she would give him this surprise picture the next time she saw him, and Mom said they were seeing him tomorrow at Grandma Faye's house.

I must hurry, Jade thought.

Knock. Knock.

"Yes, come in," said Jade.

"Jade, dinner will be ready in thirty minutes. I will call you when it is on the table, so please come downstairs, okay?"

"Okay, Mom. Do you want to see my picture? I am almost finished." She showed the picture of the angel that was almost complete.

"It is beautiful, Jade. How angelic!"

"It is for Uncle Robert. I cannot wait to give it to him!"

"He will love it, Jade."

Twenty minutes later

"Dinner!" shouted Mom.

Jade went downstairs for dinner. *Meatballs again?* she thought. Her mind said no, but deep down, she had a voice in her heart that often told her what to do. Sometimes she listened, and sometimes she did not—she called it her heart's voice. This time her heart's voice told her to eat her dinner as it would make her parents happy (and she would be making a good choice). So she did.

After telling her parents all about her day in school, she looked down at her plate and realized she ate all her veggies too! *Wow,* she thought, *my heart's voice really does help me make the right choice. Hmm.*

That night, before bed, her dad went in to say "Good night."

"Jade, I have been meaning to ask you. Have you seen my new pen I just got for my birthday?"

There was that voice again. She could hear it in her heart; it was whispering to her, "You saw the pen. You used it to draw the angel. Tell him yes."

But she thought, *What if I get in trouble? It's his new pen. He just got it. I did not ask. What if he takes away the TV and my new show is on tomorrow? Ugh.* She started sweating.

"Jade?" asked Dad. "Did you see my pen? Is there something you want to tell me, sweetheart?"

She decided to listen to her heart's voice and shouted, "Yes!"

Dad's head flung back, almost startled. "Why are you shouting?"

"Umm, I am just worried you will be mad," said Jade.

"It is okay, sweetheart. You were honest. That means more to me than anything else, just please ask first before you want to use something of mine, and always be sure to return it afterward."

"Okay, Dad. I was drawing an angel with it. It is right here, want to see?" Jade held up the picture of the angel.

"Yes. Wow, Jade! You are one talented eleven-year-old!"

"It is for Uncle Robert. I cannot wait to give it to him."

"He is going to love it, sweetheart," said Dad.

That night as Jade drifted off to sleep, she thought about her day and how each time she listened to the voice in her heart, she made the right choice. And when she didn't listen, she made the wrong choice. *What is that voice called?* she thought. *I need to find out.*

The next day after school, she ran into Grandma Faye's house, with her picture in hand. "Here, Uncle Robert! This is for you!"

He looked up after looking at her picture. "This angel is as beautiful as you, and you are one heck of an artist, Jade. Thank you, I love it! Is this in pen too? That is EVEN more impressive!" exclaimed her uncle.

17

She hugged him. "I started listening to my heart's voice, it told me you would love a picture of an angel. I'm glad I listened."

Uncle Robert laughed. "Your heart's voice? You mean your intuition. Yes, Jade, we all have it, and that's exactly what it's there for: to help guide us to make good choices. You're smart AND talented, my beautiful niece, Jade."

About the Author

Renée is a mom, a wife, a daughter, a sister, a School Counselor, and now an author of her first children's book, *Your Heart's Voice*. Renée was born and raised in New York. Renée worked as a School Counselor for ten years in New York City. She has her Master's Degrees in Counseling and School Leadership. Since having children, Renée has been home helping raise her children, ages three, six, and nine. Books are an integral part of her family's day. Luckily, all three children have a strong love for books, which helped Renée develop the idea of writing this book. Renée has always used her intuition, starting from a young age, to adulthood, to help guide her in making the right choices for her life and wanted to write this book to help remind others to use theirs.

Printed in the USA
CPSIA information can be obtained
at www.ICGtesting.com
LVHW061244240124
769621LV00015B/54